*For my darlings,
Ellody, Briar and Asher*

"There is always magic in the world
if you look for it"

Copyright © 2025 Lakely James Publishing

Written by Lakely James

Cover and internal illustrations by María Angélica Guerrero

All rights reserved. No part of this publication may be reproduced or stored in a retrieval system, or transmitted in any form or by any means, electronic, mechanical, recording, or otherwise, without written permission from its publisher, Lakely James.

The art was first sketched, then painted by hand and assembled digitally by the artist.

ISBN 978-1-7388151-1-1
ISBN 978-1-7388151-0-4
Published by Lakely James
Ilderton, Ontario, Canada

the lie we call SPRING

Written by
Lakely James

Illustrated by
María Angélica Guerrero

Each year in April,
Daddy says the same thing!
One day of warmth,
He'd exclaim, "Guys! It's spring!"
And time after time,
We'd fall for it hard:
Pull up the garden;
Clean out the yard.
Mom would watch sipping coffee,
And encourage the guy,
Silently knowing,
That spring. was. a. lie!

Canadian winters
Drag on into May.
She'd remind him of this
Throughout April each day.

And yet, the excitement
Of hot summer rays,
The smell on the cusp
Of those sweet-smelling days,
Would cloud all our judgement.
We'd frolic and play;

Side with dear dad,
And put our snowsuits away.

But as if she were listening,
This cunning girl "Spring,"
Waiting just as we finished
Jamming the last mitten in.
And putting the trunk
Of jackets top shelf,
From out of the blue...

Dropped a snowflake itself!

Then down poured the snow
In big heavy mounds.

Out came the winds,
'til snow covered the ground.

And it was our fault;
WE put the snowsuits away!

Then days later again
The sun would appear,
And again he'd exclaim,
"Spring guys! It's here!"
And forgetting what happened
Saturday past,
We'd get out the bikes,
And make the day last!

Breathing in nature,
The earth came alive!

Birds chirped in trees;
Blue filled the sky.
Confident that spring,
Was now here to stay,

We cleaned up the blower
And put it away...

Yet, watching intently,
And sly as a fox,
Snow jumped on us all
As if out of a box!
Down poured the snow
In big heavy mounds.
Out came the winds,
'til snow covered the ground.

God bless him, our dad,
For the next summer day,
You guessed it, uh huh,
"Spring's here to stay!"
Mom stifled her grin
With eyes looking low.
Catching her laugh,
What did she know?
The distraction was minor;
We were opening the pool!
Today was the day
Right after school!

On the play yard we skipped,

Wrote with our chalk,

Mounted the climbers,

Went out for a walk.

We dug in the sand,

And stared at the sun,

Played hopscotch and chase.
Freezies! What fun!

And when the day ended,
Straight home from school,
We ran to the back,
And jumped in our pool...

But then, there it was,
Right there on que.
"Spring" came about!
It was what our mom knew.
Mid-splash we froze,
As the winds changed to cold,
And frozen in water,
Of us made a mold!

Next year, I won't listen
To hopefuls alike.
I won't pack-up or dally,
Nor jump on my bike.
No ice creams or sundaes,
Nor hopscotch too soon.
From now on no putting
Away things 'til June!

www.ingramcontent.com/pod-product-compliance
Lightning Source LLC
Chambersburg PA
CBHW042128040426
42450CB00002B/117